RECORD OF EVENTS

DATE _____ TIME _____

GW01454420

WHO _____ WHAT _____ WHERE _____

HAIR _____ MALE / FEMALE / ANIMAL _____

CAR _____ BIKE _____ FOOT/OTHER (Bus- etc.) _____

CLOTHS _____

EXTRA NOTES/OBSERVATIONS ETC

_____

_____

_____

_____

_____

_____

_____

_____

RECORD OF EVENTS

DATE _____ TIME _____ PLACE _____

WHO_____ WHAT_____ WHERE _____

HAIR_____ MALE / FEMALE / ANIMAL _____

CAR_____ BIKE_____ FOOT/OTHER (Bus- etc.)_____

CLOTHS _____

EXTRA NOTES/OBSERVATIONS ETC

_____

_____

_____

_____

_____

_____

_____

_____

RECORD OF EVENTS

DATE _____ TIME _____ PLACE _____

WHO _____ WHAT _____ WHERE _____

HAIR _____ MALE / FEMALE / ANIMAL _____

CAR _____ BIKE _____ FOOT/OTHER (Bus- etc.) _____

CLOTHS _____

EXTRA NOTES/OBSERVATIONS ETC

_____

_____

_____

_____

_____

_____

_____

_____

RECORD OF EVENTS

DATE _____ TIME _____ PLACE _____

WHO_____WHAT_____WHERE _____

HAIR_____MALE / FEMALE / ANIMAL _____

CAR_____ BIKE_____FOOT/OTHER **(Bus- etc.)**_____

CLOTHS_____

EXTRA NOTES/OBSERVATIONS ETC

_____

_____

_____

_____

_____

_____

_____

_____

RECORD OF EVENTS

DATE _____ TIME _____ PLACE _____

WHO_____WHAT_____WHERE _____

HAIR_____MALE / FEMALE / ANIMAL _____

CAR_____ BIKE _____FOOT/OTHER **(Bus- etc.)**_____

CLOTHS _____

EXTRA NOTES/OBSERVATIONS ETC

_____

_____

_____

_____

_____

_____

_____

_____

RECORD OF EVENTS

DATE _____ TIME _____ PLACE _____

WHO_____WHAT_____WHERE _____

HAIR_____MALE / FEMALE / ANIMAL _____

CAR_____BIKE_____FOOT/OTHER (Bus- etc.)_____

CLOTHS _____

EXTRA NOTES/OBSERVATIONS ETC

_____

_____

_____

_____

_____

_____

_____

_____

RECORD OF EVENTS

DATE _____ TIME _____ PLACE _____

WHO _____ WHAT _____ WHERE _____

HAIR _____ MALE / FEMALE / ANIMAL _____

CAR _____ BIKE _____ FOOT/OTHER (Bus- etc.) _____

CLOTHS _____

EXTRA NOTES/OBSERVATIONS ETC

_____

_____

_____

_____

_____

_____

_____

_____

RECORD OF EVENTS

DATE _____ TIME _____ PLACE _____

WHO_____ WHAT_____ WHERE _____

HAIR_____ MALE / FEMALE / ANIMAL _____

CAR_____ BIKE_____ FOOT/OTHER^(Bus- etc.)_____

CLOTHS_____

EXTRA NOTES/OBSERVATIONS ETC

_____

_____

_____

_____

_____

_____

_____

_____

_____

RECORD OF EVENTS

DATE _____ TIME _____ PLACE _____

WHO_____WHAT_____WHERE _____

HAIR_____MALE / FEMALE / ANIMAL _____

CAR_____ BIKE_____FOOT/OTHER (Bus- etc.)_____

CLOTHS _____

EXTRA NOTES/OBSERVATIONS ETC

_____

_____

_____

_____

_____

_____

_____

_____

RECORD OF EVENTS

DATE _____ TIME _____ PLACE _____

WHO _____ WHAT _____ WHERE _____

HAIR _____ MALE / FEMALE / ANIMAL _____

CAR _____ BIKE _____ FOOT/OTHER (Bus- etc.) _____

CLOTHS _____

EXTRA NOTES/OBSERVATIONS ETC

_____

_____

_____

_____

_____

_____

_____

RECORD OF EVENTS

DATE _____ TIME _____ PLACE _____

WHO_____ WHAT_____ WHERE _____

HAIR_____ MALE / FEMALE / ANIMAL _____

CAR_____ BIKE_____ FOOT/OTHER_____ (Bus- etc.)

CLOTHS _____

EXTRA NOTES/OBSERVATIONS ETC

_____

_____

_____

_____

_____

_____

_____

_____

_____

RECORD OF EVENTS

DATE _____ TIME _____ PLACE _____

WHO _____ WHAT _____ WHERE _____

HAIR _____ MALE / FEMALE / ANIMAL _____

CAR _____ BIKE _____ FOOT/OTHER **(Bus- etc.)** _____

CLOTHS _____

EXTRA NOTES/OBSERVATIONS ETC

_____

_____

_____

_____

_____

_____

_____

_____

RECORD OF EVENTS

DATE _____ TIME _____ PLACE _____

WHO _____ WHAT _____ WHERE _____

HAIR _____ MALE / FEMALE / ANIMAL _____

CAR _____ BIKE _____ FOOT/OTHER (Bus- etc.) _____

CLOTHS _____

EXTRA NOTES/OBSERVATIONS ETC

_____

_____

_____

_____

_____

_____

_____

_____

_____

RECORD OF EVENTS

DATE _____ TIME _____ PLACE _____

WHO_____ WHAT_____ WHERE _____

HAIR_____ MALE / FEMALE / ANIMAL _____

CAR_____ BIKE_____ FOOT/OTHER **(Bus- etc.)**_____

CLOTHS _____

EXTRA NOTES/OBSERVATIONS ETC

_____

_____

_____

_____

_____

_____

_____

_____

_____

RECORD OF EVENTS

DATE _____ TIME _____ PLACE _____

WHO _____ WHAT _____ WHERE _____

HAIR _____ MALE / FEMALE / ANIMAL _____

CAR _____ BIKE _____ FOOT/OTHER (Bus- etc.) _____

CLOTHS _____

EXTRA NOTES/OBSERVATIONS ETC

_____

_____

_____

_____

_____

_____

_____

_____

RECORD OF EVENTS

DATE _____ TIME _____ PLACE _____

WHO_____WHAT_____WHERE _____

HAIR_____MALE / FEMALE / ANIMAL _____

CAR_____ BIKE_____FOOT/OTHER **(Bus- etc.)**_____

CLOTHS _____

EXTRA NOTES/OBSERVATIONS ETC

_____

_____

_____

_____

_____

_____

_____

_____

_____

RECORD OF EVENTS

DATE _____ TIME _____ PLACE _____

WHO_____ WHAT_____ WHERE _____

HAIR_____ MALE / FEMALE / ANIMAL _____

CAR_____ BIKE_____ FOOT/OTHER (Bus- etc.) _____

CLOTHS _____

EXTRA NOTES/OBSERVATIONS ETC

_____

_____

_____

_____

_____

_____

_____

_____

RECORD OF EVENTS

DATE _____ TIME _____ PLACE _____

WHO_____ WHAT_____ WHERE _____

HAIR_____ MALE / FEMALE / ANIMAL _____

CAR_____ BIKE_____ **(Bus- etc.)** FOOT/OTHER_____

CLOTHS _____

EXTRA NOTES/OBSERVATIONS ETC

_____

_____

_____

_____

_____

_____

_____

_____

RECORD OF EVENTS

DATE _____ TIME _____ PLACE _____

WHO _____ WHAT _____ WHERE _____

HAIR _____ MALE / FEMALE / ANIMAL _____

CAR _____ BIKE _____ FOOT/OTHER (Bus- etc.) _____

CLOTHS _____

EXTRA NOTES/OBSERVATIONS ETC

_____

_____

_____

_____

_____

_____

_____

_____

_____

RECORD OF EVENTS

DATE _____ TIME _____ PLACE _____

WHO _____ WHAT _____ WHERE _____

HAIR _____ MALE / FEMALE / ANIMAL _____

CAR _____ BIKE _____ FOOT/OTHER _____ (Bus- etc.)

CLOTHS _____

EXTRA NOTES/OBSERVATIONS ETC

_____

_____

_____

_____

_____

_____

_____

_____

RECORD OF EVENTS

DATE _____ TIME _____ PLACE _____

WHO_____ WHAT_____ WHERE _____

HAIR_____ MALE / FEMALE / ANIMAL _____

CAR_____ BIKE_____ FOOT/OTHER (Bus- etc.) _____

CLOTHS _____

EXTRA NOTES/OBSERVATIONS ETC

_____

_____

_____

_____

_____

_____

_____

_____

RECORD OF EVENTS

DATE _____ TIME _____ PLACE _____

WHO_____ WHAT_____ WHERE _____

HAIR_____MALE / FEMALE / ANIMAL _____

CAR_____ BIKE_____FOOT/OTHER^(Bus- etc.)_____

CLOTHS _____

EXTRA NOTES/OBSERVATIONS ETC

_____

_____

_____

_____

_____

_____

_____

_____

RECORD OF EVENTS

DATE _____ TIME _____ PLACE _____

WHO_____WHAT_____WHERE _____

HAIR_____MALE / FEMALE / ANIMAL _____

CAR_____ BIKE_____FOOT/OTHER (Bus- etc.)_____

CLOTHS _____

EXTRA NOTES/OBSERVATIONS ETC

_____

_____

_____

_____

_____

_____

_____

RECORD OF EVENTS

DATE _____ TIME _____ PLACE _____

WHO _____ WHAT _____ WHERE _____

HAIR _____ MALE / FEMALE / ANIMAL _____

CAR _____ BIKE _____ FOOT/OTHER (Bus- etc.) _____

CLOTHS _____

EXTRA NOTES/OBSERVATIONS ETC

_____

_____

_____

_____

_____

_____

_____

RECORD OF EVENTS

DATE _____ TIME _____ PLACE _____

WHO _____ WHAT _____ WHERE _____

HAIR _____ MALE / FEMALE / ANIMAL _____

CAR _____ BIKE _____ FOOT/OTHER _____ **(Bus- etc.)**

CLOTHS _____

EXTRA NOTES/OBSERVATIONS ETC

_____

_____

_____

_____

_____

_____

_____

_____

RECORD OF EVENTS

DATE _____ TIME _____ PLACE _____

WHO_____ WHAT_____ WHERE _____

HAIR_____ MALE / FEMALE / ANIMAL _____

CAR_____ BIKE_____ FOOT/OTHER (Bus- etc.)_____

CLOTHS _____

EXTRA NOTES/OBSERVATIONS ETC

_____

_____

_____

_____

_____

_____

_____

RECORD OF EVENTS

DATE _____ TIME _____ PLACE _____

WHO_____WHAT_____WHERE _____

HAIR_____MALE / FEMALE / ANIMAL _____

CAR_____ BIKE_____FOOT/OTHER_____ (Bus- etc.)

CLOTHS _____

EXTRA NOTES/OBSERVATIONS ETC

_____

_____

_____

_____

_____

_____

_____

_____

RECORD OF EVENTS

DATE _____ TIME _____ PLACE _____

WHO_____WHAT_____WHERE _____

HAIR_____MALE / FEMALE / ANIMAL _____

CAR_____ BIKE_____FOOT/OTHER **(Bus- etc.)** _____

CLOTHS _____

EXTRA NOTES/OBSERVATIONS ETC

_____

_____

_____

_____

_____

_____

_____

_____

RECORD OF EVENTS

DATE _____ TIME _____ PLACE _____

WHO _____ WHAT _____ WHERE _____

HAIR _____ MALE / FEMALE / ANIMAL _____

CAR _____ BIKE _____ FOOT/OTHER _____ (Bus- etc.)

CLOTHS _____

EXTRA NOTES/OBSERVATIONS ETC

_____

_____

_____

_____

_____

_____

_____

_____

RECORD OF EVENTS

DATE _____ TIME _____ PLACE _____

WHO_____ WHAT_____ WHERE _____

HAIR_____ MALE / FEMALE / ANIMAL _____

CAR_____ BIKE_____ FOOT/OTHER_____ (Bus- etc.)

CLOTHS _____

EXTRA NOTES/OBSERVATIONS ETC

_____

_____

_____

_____

_____

_____

_____

_____

RECORD OF EVENTS

DATE _____ TIME _____ PLACE _____

WHO_____ WHAT_____ WHERE _____

HAIR_____MALE / FEMALE / ANIMAL _____

CAR_____ BIKE_____ FOOT/OTHER^(Bus- etc.)_____

CLOTHS _____

EXTRA NOTES/OBSERVATIONS ETC

_____

_____

_____

_____

_____

_____

_____

_____

RECORD OF EVENTS

DATE _____ TIME _____ PLACE _____

WHO_____ WHAT_____ WHERE _____

HAIR_____ MALE / FEMALE / ANIMAL _____

CAR_____ BIKE_____ FOOT/OTHER **(Bus- etc.)**_____

CLOTHS _____

EXTRA NOTES/OBSERVATIONS ETC

_____

_____

_____

_____

_____

_____

_____

_____

RECORD OF EVENTS

DATE _____ TIME _____ PLACE _____

WHO_____ WHAT_____ WHERE _____

HAIR_____MALE / FEMALE / ANIMAL _____

CAR_____ BIKE_____FOOT/OTHER **(Bus- etc.)**_____

CLOTHS _____

EXTRA NOTES/OBSERVATIONS ETC

_____

_____

_____

_____

_____

_____

_____

_____

RECORD OF EVENTS

DATE _____ TIME _____ PLACE _____

WHO _____ WHAT _____ WHERE _____

HAIR _____ MALE / FEMALE / ANIMAL _____

CAR _____ BIKE _____ FOOT/OTHER **(Bus- etc.)** _____

CLOTHS _____

EXTRA NOTES/OBSERVATIONS ETC

_____

_____

_____

_____

_____

_____

_____

_____

RECORD OF EVENTS

DATE _____ TIME _____ PLACE _____

WHO_____ WHAT_____ WHERE _____

HAIR_____ MALE / FEMALE / ANIMAL _____

CAR_____ BIKE_____ FOOT/OTHER_____ (Bus- etc.)

CLOTHS _____

EXTRA NOTES/OBSERVATIONS ETC

_____

_____

_____

_____

_____

_____

_____

_____

RECORD OF EVENTS

DATE _____ TIME _____ PLACE _____

WHO_____WHAT_____WHERE _____

HAIR_____MALE / FEMALE / ANIMAL _____

CAR_____ BIKE_____FOOT/OTHER **(Bus- etc.)**_____

CLOTHS _____

EXTRA NOTES/OBSERVATIONS ETC

_____

_____

_____

_____

_____

_____

_____

_____

RECORD OF EVENTS

DATE _____ TIME _____ PLACE _____

WHO_____WHAT_____WHERE _____

HAIR_____MALE / FEMALE / ANIMAL _____

CAR_____ BIKE_____FOOT/OTHER_____ (Bus- etc.)

CLOTHS _____

EXTRA NOTES/OBSERVATIONS ETC

_____

_____

_____

_____

_____

_____

_____

_____

RECORD OF EVENTS

DATE _____ TIME _____ PLACE _____

WHO_____WHAT_____WHERE _____

HAIR_____MALE / FEMALE / ANIMAL _____

CAR_____ BIKE_____FOOT/OTHER (Bus- etc.)_____

CLOTHS _____

EXTRA NOTES/OBSERVATIONS ETC

_____

_____

_____

_____

_____

_____

_____

RECORD OF EVENTS

DATE _____ TIME _____ PLACE _____

WHO _____ WHAT _____ WHERE _____

HAIR _____ MALE / FEMALE / ANIMAL _____

CAR _____ BIKE _____ FOOT/OTHER (Bus- etc.) _____

CLOTHS _____

EXTRA NOTES/OBSERVATIONS ETC

_____

_____

_____

_____

_____

_____

_____

_____

RECORD OF EVENTS

DATE _____ TIME _____ PLACE _____

WHO_____ WHAT_____ WHERE _____

HAIR_____ MALE / FEMALE / ANIMAL _____

CAR_____ BIKE_____ FOOT/OTHER (Bus- etc.) _____

CLOTHS _____

EXTRA NOTES/OBSERVATIONS ETC

_____

_____

_____

_____

_____

_____

_____

RECORD OF EVENTS

DATE _____ TIME _____ PLACE _____

WHO_____WHAT_____WHERE _____

HAIR_____MALE / FEMALE / ANIMAL _____

CAR_____ BIKE_____FOOT/OTHER_____ (Bus- etc.)

CLOTHS _____

EXTRA NOTES/OBSERVATIONS ETC

_____

_____

_____

_____

_____

_____

_____

_____

RECORD OF EVENTS

DATE _____ TIME _____ PLACE _____

WHO _____ WHAT _____ WHERE _____

HAIR _____ MALE / FEMALE / ANIMAL _____

CAR _____ BIKE _____ FOOT/OTHER (Bus- etc.) _____

CLOTHS _____

EXTRA NOTES/OBSERVATIONS ETC

_____

_____

_____

_____

_____

_____

_____

RECORD OF EVENTS

DATE _____ TIME _____ PLACE _____

WHO_____WHAT_____WHERE _____

HAIR_____MALE / FEMALE / ANIMAL _____

CAR_____ BIKE_____FOOT/OTHER (Bus- etc.)_____

CLOTHS _____

EXTRA NOTES/OBSERVATIONS ETC

_____

_____

_____

_____

_____

_____

_____

_____

RECORD OF EVENTS

DATE _____ TIME _____ PLACE _____

WHO _____ WHAT _____ WHERE _____

HAIR _____ MALE / FEMALE / ANIMAL _____

CAR _____ BIKE _____ **(Bus- etc.)** FOOT/OTHER _____

CLOTHS _____

EXTRA NOTES/OBSERVATIONS ETC

_____

_____

_____

_____

_____

_____

_____

_____

RECORD OF EVENTS

DATE _____ TIME _____ PLACE _____

WHO _____ WHAT _____ WHERE _____

HAIR _____ MALE / FEMALE / ANIMAL _____

CAR _____ BIKE _____ FOOT/OTHER _____ (Bus- etc.)

CLOTHS _____

EXTRA NOTES/OBSERVATIONS ETC

_____

_____

_____

_____

_____

_____

_____

_____

RECORD OF EVENTS

DATE _____ TIME _____ PLACE _____

WHO_____ WHAT_____ WHERE _____

HAIR_____ MALE / FEMALE / ANIMAL _____

CAR_____ BIKE_____ FOOT/OTHER (Bus- etc.)_____

CLOTHS _____

EXTRA NOTES/OBSERVATIONS ETC

_____

_____

_____

_____

_____

_____

_____

RECORD OF EVENTS

DATE _____ TIME _____ PLACE _____

WHO_____WHAT_____WHERE _____

HAIR_____MALE / FEMALE / ANIMAL _____

CAR_____ BIKE_____FOOT/OTHER**(Bus- etc.)**_____

CLOTHS _____

EXTRA NOTES/OBSERVATIONS ETC

_____

_____

_____

_____

_____

_____

_____

_____

RECORD OF EVENTS

DATE _____ TIME _____ PLACE _____

WHO _____ WHAT _____ WHERE _____

HAIR _____ MALE / FEMALE / ANIMAL _____

CAR _____ BIKE _____ **(Bus- etc.)** FOOT/OTHER _____

CLOTHS _____

EXTRA NOTES/OBSERVATIONS ETC

_____

_____

_____

_____

_____

_____

_____

_____

RECORD OF EVENTS

DATE _____ TIME _____ PLACE _____

WHO_____WHAT_____WHERE _____

HAIR_____MALE / FEMALE / ANIMAL _____

CAR_____ BIKE_____FOOT/OTHER (Bus- etc.)_____

CLOTHS _____

EXTRA NOTES/OBSERVATIONS ETC

_____

_____

_____

_____

_____

_____

_____

_____

RECORD OF EVENTS

DATE _____ TIME _____ PLACE _____

WHO _____ WHAT _____ WHERE _____

HAIR _____ MALE / FEMALE / ANIMAL _____

CAR _____ BIKE _____ FOOT/OTHER **(Bus- etc.)** _____

CLOTHS _____

EXTRA NOTES/OBSERVATIONS ETC

_____

_____

_____

_____

_____

_____

_____

_____

RECORD OF EVENTS

DATE _____ TIME _____ PLACE _____

WHO _____ WHAT _____ WHERE _____

HAIR _____ MALE / FEMALE / ANIMAL _____

CAR _____ BIKE _____ FOOT/OTHER **(Bus- etc.)** _____

CLOTHS _____

EXTRA NOTES/OBSERVATIONS ETC

_____

_____

_____

_____

_____

_____

_____

_____

RECORD OF EVENTS

DATE _____ TIME _____ PLACE _____

WHO_____ WHAT_____ WHERE _____

HAIR_____ MALE / FEMALE / ANIMAL _____

CAR_____ BIKE_____ **(Bus- etc.)** FOOT/OTHER_____

CLOTHS _____

EXTRA NOTES/OBSERVATIONS ETC

_____

_____

_____

_____

_____

_____

_____

_____

RECORD OF EVENTS

DATE _____ TIME _____ PLACE _____

WHO _____ WHAT _____ WHERE _____

HAIR _____ MALE / FEMALE / ANIMAL _____

CAR _____ BIKE _____ FOOT/OTHER _____ (Bus- etc.)

CLOTHS _____

EXTRA NOTES/OBSERVATIONS ETC

_____

_____

_____

_____

_____

_____

_____

_____

RECORD OF EVENTS

DATE _____ TIME _____ PLACE _____

WHO_____ WHAT_____ WHERE _____

HAIR_____ MALE / FEMALE / ANIMAL _____

CAR_____ BIKE_____ FOOT/OTHER **(Bus- etc.)**_____

CLOTHS _____

EXTRA NOTES/OBSERVATIONS ETC

_____

_____

_____

_____

_____

_____

_____

_____

RECORD OF EVENTS

DATE _____ TIME _____ PLACE _____

WHO_____WHAT_____WHERE _____

HAIR_____MALE / FEMALE / ANIMAL _____

CAR_____ BIKE _____FOOT/OTHER**(Bus- etc.)**_____

CLOTHS _____

EXTRA NOTES/OBSERVATIONS ETC

_____

_____

_____

_____

_____

_____

_____

_____

RECORD OF EVENTS

DATE _____ TIME _____ PLACE _____

WHO_____ WHAT_____ WHERE _____

HAIR_____ MALE / FEMALE / ANIMAL _____

CAR_____ BIKE_____FOOT/OTHER (Bus- etc.)_____

CLOTHS _____

EXTRA NOTES/OBSERVATIONS ETC

_____

_____

_____

_____

_____

_____

_____

_____

RECORD OF EVENTS

DATE _____ TIME _____ PLACE _____

WHO_____WHAT_____WHERE _____

HAIR_____MALE / FEMALE / ANIMAL _____

CAR_____ BIKE_____FOOT/OTHER (Bus- etc.)_____

CLOTHS _____

EXTRA NOTES/OBSERVATIONS ETC

_____

_____

_____

_____

_____

_____

_____

_____

RECORD OF EVENTS

DATE _____ TIME _____ PLACE _____

WHO_____ WHAT_____WHERE _____

HAIR_____MALE / FEMALE / ANIMAL _____

CAR_____ BIKE _____FOOT/OTHER^(Bus- etc.)_____

CLOTHS _____

EXTRA NOTES/OBSERVATIONS ETC

_____

_____

_____

_____

_____

_____

_____

_____

RECORD OF EVENTS

DATE _____ TIME _____ PLACE _____

WHO _____ WHAT _____ WHERE _____

HAIR _____ MALE / FEMALE / ANIMAL _____

CAR _____ BIKE _____ FOOT/OTHER _____ (Bus- etc.)

CLOTHS _____

EXTRA NOTES/OBSERVATIONS ETC

_____

_____

_____

_____

_____

_____

_____

_____

RECORD OF EVENTS

DATE _____ TIME _____ PLACE _____

WHO_____WHAT_____WHERE _____

HAIR_____MALE / FEMALE / ANIMAL _____

CAR_____ BIKE_____FOOT/OTHER (Bus- etc.)_____

CLOTHS _____

EXTRA NOTES/OBSERVATIONS ETC

_____

_____

_____

_____

_____

_____

_____

_____

RECORD OF EVENTS

DATE _____ TIME _____ PLACE _____

WHO_____WHAT_____WHERE _____

HAIR_____MALE / FEMALE / ANIMAL _____

CAR_____ BIKE_____FOOT/OTHER (Bus- etc.) _____

CLOTHS _____

EXTRA NOTES/OBSERVATIONS ETC

_____

_____

_____

_____

_____

_____

_____

_____

RECORD OF EVENTS

DATE _____ TIME _____ PLACE _____

WHO_____WHAT_____WHERE _____

HAIR_____MALE / FEMALE / ANIMAL _____

CAR_____ BIKE_____FOOT/OTHER**(Bus- etc.)**_____

CLOTHS _____

EXTRA NOTES/OBSERVATIONS ETC

_____

_____

_____

_____

_____

_____

_____

_____

RECORD OF EVENTS

DATE _____ TIME _____ PLACE _____

WHO_____WHAT_____WHERE _____

HAIR_____MALE / FEMALE / ANIMAL _____

CAR_____ BIKE _____FOOT/OTHER (Bus- etc.)_____

CLOTHS _____

EXTRA NOTES/OBSERVATIONS ETC

_____

_____

_____

_____

_____

_____

_____

_____

_____

RECORD OF EVENTS

DATE _____ TIME _____ PLACE _____

WHO _____ WHAT _____ WHERE _____

HAIR _____ MALE / FEMALE / ANIMAL _____

CAR _____ BIKE _____ FOOT/OTHER **(Bus- etc.)** _____

CLOTHS _____

EXTRA NOTES/OBSERVATIONS ETC

_____

_____

_____

_____

_____

_____

_____

_____

RECORD OF EVENTS

DATE _____ TIME _____ PLACE _____

WHO _____ WHAT _____ WHERE _____

HAIR _____ MALE / FEMALE / ANIMAL _____

CAR _____ BIKE _____ FOOT/OTHER _____
(Bus- etc.)

CLOTHS _____

EXTRA NOTES/OBSERVATIONS ETC

_____

_____

_____

_____

_____

_____

_____

_____

RECORD OF EVENTS

DATE _____ TIME _____ PLACE _____

WHO _____ WHAT _____ WHERE _____

HAIR _____ MALE / FEMALE / ANIMAL _____

CAR _____ BIKE _____ FOOT/OTHER **(Bus- etc.)** _____

CLOTHS _____

EXTRA NOTES/OBSERVATIONS ETC

_____

_____

_____

_____

_____

_____

_____

_____

RECORD OF EVENTS

DATE _____ TIME _____ PLACE _____

WHO_____WHAT_____WHERE _____

HAIR_____MALE/FEMALE/ANIMAL _____

CAR_____ BIKE_____FOOT/OTHER (Bus- etc.)_____

CLOTHS _____

EXTRA NOTES/OBSERVATIONS ETC

_____

_____

_____

_____

_____

_____

_____

_____

RECORD OF EVENTS

DATE _____ TIME _____ PLACE _____

WHO _____ WHAT _____ WHERE _____

HAIR _____ MALE / FEMALE / ANIMAL _____

CAR _____ BIKE _____ FOOT/OTHER^(Bus- etc.) _____

CLOTHS _____

EXTRA NOTES/OBSERVATIONS ETC

_____

_____

_____

_____

_____

_____

_____

_____

RECORD OF EVENTS

DATE _____ TIME _____ PLACE _____

WHO_____ WHAT_____ WHERE _____

HAIR_____ MALE / FEMALE / ANIMAL _____

CAR_____ BIKE_____ FOOT/OTHER **(Bus- etc.)**_____

CLOTHS _____

EXTRA NOTES/OBSERVATIONS ETC

_____

_____

_____

_____

_____

_____

_____

_____

RECORD OF EVENTS

DATE _____ TIME _____ PLACE _____

WHO _____ WHAT _____ WHERE _____

HAIR _____ MALE / FEMALE / ANIMAL _____

CAR _____ BIKE _____ FOOT/OTHER (Bus- etc.) _____

CLOTHS _____

EXTRA NOTES/OBSERVATIONS ETC

_____

_____

_____

_____

_____

_____

_____

_____

RECORD OF EVENTS

DATE _____ TIME _____ PLACE _____

WHO _____ WHAT _____ WHERE _____

HAIR _____ MALE / FEMALE / ANIMAL _____

CAR _____ BIKE _____ FOOT/OTHER (Bus- etc.) _____

CLOTHS _____

EXTRA NOTES/OBSERVATIONS ETC

_____

_____

_____

_____

_____

_____

_____

_____

RECORD OF EVENTS

DATE _____ TIME _____ PLACE _____

WHO _____ WHAT _____ WHERE _____

HAIR _____ MALE / FEMALE / ANIMAL _____

CAR _____ BIKE _____ FOOT/OTHER (Bus- etc.) _____

CLOTHS _____

EXTRA NOTES/OBSERVATIONS ETC

_____

_____

_____

_____

_____

_____

_____

_____

RECORD OF EVENTS

DATE _____ TIME _____ PLACE _____

WHO_____WHAT_____WHERE _____

HAIR_____MALE / FEMALE / ANIMAL _____

CAR_____ BIKE_____FOOT/OTHER (Bus- etc.)_____

CLOTHS _____

EXTRA NOTES/OBSERVATIONS ETC

_____

_____

_____

_____

_____

_____

_____

_____

RECORD OF EVENTS

DATE _____ TIME _____ PLACE _____

WHO_____ WHAT_____ WHERE _____

HAIR_____ MALE / FEMALE / ANIMAL _____

CAR_____ BIKE_____ FOOT/OTHER_____ (Bus- etc.)

CLOTHS _____

EXTRA NOTES/OBSERVATIONS ETC

_____

_____

_____

_____

_____

_____

_____

_____

RECORD OF EVENTS

DATE _____ TIME _____ PLACE _____

WHO_____WHAT_____WHERE _____

HAIR_____MALE / FEMALE / ANIMAL _____

CAR_____ BIKE_____FOOT/OTHER (Bus- etc.)_____

CLOTHS _____

EXTRA NOTES/OBSERVATIONS ETC

_____

_____

_____

_____

_____

_____

_____

_____

RECORD OF EVENTS

DATE _____ TIME _____ PLACE _____

WHO _____ WHAT _____ WHERE _____

HAIR _____ MALE / FEMALE / ANIMAL _____

CAR _____ BIKE _____ FOOT/OTHER **(Bus- etc.)** _____

CLOTHS _____

EXTRA NOTES/OBSERVATIONS ETC

_____

_____

_____

_____

_____

_____

_____

_____

RECORD OF EVENTS

DATE _____ TIME _____ PLACE _____

WHO _____ WHAT _____ WHERE _____

HAIR _____ MALE / FEMALE / ANIMAL _____

CAR _____ BIKE _____ FOOT/OTHER (Bus- etc.) _____

CLOTHS _____

EXTRA NOTES/OBSERVATIONS ETC

_____

_____

_____

_____

_____

_____

_____

_____

RECORD OF EVENTS

DATE _____ TIME _____ PLACE _____

WHO _____ WHAT _____ WHERE _____

HAIR _____ MALE / FEMALE / ANIMAL _____

CAR _____ BIKE _____ FOOT/OTHER (Bus- etc.) _____

CLOTHS _____

EXTRA NOTES/OBSERVATIONS ETC

_____

_____

_____

_____

_____

_____

_____

_____

RECORD OF EVENTS

DATE _____ TIME _____ PLACE _____

WHO_____ WHAT_____ WHERE _____

HAIR_____ MALE / FEMALE / ANIMAL _____

CAR_____ BIKE_____ FOOT/OTHER_____ **(Bus- etc.)**

CLOTHS _____

EXTRA NOTES/OBSERVATIONS ETC

_____

_____

_____

_____

_____

_____

_____

_____

RECORD OF EVENTS

DATE _____ TIME _____ PLACE _____

WHO _____ WHAT _____ WHERE _____

HAIR _____ MALE / FEMALE / ANIMAL _____

CAR _____ BIKE _____ FOOT/OTHER (Bus- etc.) _____

CLOTHS _____

EXTRA NOTES/OBSERVATIONS ETC

_____

_____

_____

_____

_____

_____

_____

_____

RECORD OF EVENTS

DATE _____ TIME _____ PLACE _____

WHO _____ WHAT _____ WHERE _____

HAIR _____ MALE / FEMALE / ANIMAL _____

CAR _____ BIKE _____ FOOT/OTHER (Bus- etc.) _____

CLOTHS _____

EXTRA NOTES/OBSERVATIONS ETC

_____

_____

_____

_____

_____

_____

_____

_____

RECORD OF EVENTS

DATE _____ TIME _____ PLACE _____

WHO_____ WHAT_____ WHERE _____

HAIR_____ MALE / FEMALE / ANIMAL _____

CAR_____ BIKE_____ FOOT/OTHER_____
(Bus- etc.)

CLOTHS _____

EXTRA NOTES/OBSERVATIONS ETC

_____

_____

_____

_____

_____

_____

_____

_____

RECORD OF EVENTS

DATE _____ TIME _____ PLACE _____

WHO_____ WHAT_____ WHERE _____

HAIR_____ MALE / FEMALE / ANIMAL _____

CAR_____ BIKE_____ FOOT/OTHER^(Bus- etc.)_____

CLOTHS _____

EXTRA NOTES/OBSERVATIONS ETC

_____

_____

_____

_____

_____

_____

_____

_____

RECORD OF EVENTS

DATE _____ TIME _____ PLACE _____

WHO _____ WHAT _____ WHERE _____

HAIR _____ MALE / FEMALE / ANIMAL _____

CAR _____ BIKE _____ FOOT/OTHER **(Bus- etc.)** _____

CLOTHS _____

EXTRA NOTES/OBSERVATIONS ETC

_____

_____

_____

_____

_____

_____

_____

_____

RECORD OF EVENTS

DATE _____ TIME _____ PLACE _____

WHO_____ WHAT_____ WHERE _____

HAIR_____MALE / FEMALE / ANIMAL _____

CAR_____ BIKE_____FOOT/OTHER _____
(Bus- etc.)

CLOTHS _____

EXTRA NOTES/OBSERVATIONS ETC

_____

_____

_____

_____

_____

_____

_____

_____

RECORD OF EVENTS

DATE _____ TIME _____ PLACE _____

WHO _____ WHAT _____ WHERE _____

HAIR _____ MALE / FEMALE / ANIMAL _____

CAR _____ BIKE _____ FOOT/OTHER _____
(Bus- etc.)

CLOTHS _____

EXTRA NOTES/OBSERVATIONS ETC

_____

_____

_____

_____

_____

_____

_____

_____

RECORD OF EVENTS

DATE _____ TIME _____ PLACE _____

WHO _____ WHAT _____ WHERE _____

HAIR _____ MALE / FEMALE / ANIMAL _____

CAR _____ BIKE _____ FOOT/OTHER (Bus- etc.) _____

CLOTHS _____

EXTRA NOTES/OBSERVATIONS ETC

_____

_____

_____

_____

_____

_____

_____

_____

RECORD OF EVENTS

DATE _____ TIME _____ PLACE _____

WHO _____ WHAT _____ WHERE _____

HAIR _____ MALE / FEMALE / ANIMAL _____

CAR _____ BIKE _____ FOOT/OTHER (Bus- etc.) _____

CLOTHS _____

EXTRA NOTES/OBSERVATIONS ETC

_____

_____

_____

_____

_____

_____

_____

_____

RECORD OF EVENTS

DATE _____ TIME _____ PLACE _____

WHO_____ WHAT_____ WHERE _____

HAIR_____ MALE / FEMALE / ANIMAL _____

CAR_____ BIKE_____ FOOT/OTHER_____
                                            (Bus- etc.)

CLOTHS _____

EXTRA NOTES/OBSERVATIONS ETC

_____

_____

_____

_____

_____

_____

_____

_____

RECORD OF EVENTS

DATE _____ TIME _____ PLACE _____

WHO_____ WHAT_____ WHERE _____

HAIR_____ MALE / FEMALE / ANIMAL _____

CAR_____ BIKE_____ FOOT/OTHER (Bus- etc.)_____

CLOTHS _____

EXTRA NOTES/OBSERVATIONS ETC

_____

_____

_____

_____

_____

_____

_____

_____

RECORD OF EVENTS

DATE _____ TIME _____ PLACE _____

WHO_____ WHAT_____ WHERE _____

HAIR_____MALE / FEMALE / ANIMAL _____

CAR_____ BIKE_____FOOT/OTHER (Bus- etc.)_____

CLOTHS _____

EXTRA NOTES/OBSERVATIONS ETC

_____

_____

_____

_____

_____

_____

_____

_____

RECORD OF EVENTS

DATE _____ TIME _____ PLACE _____

WHO_____ WHAT_____ WHERE _____

HAIR_____ MALE / FEMALE / ANIMAL _____

CAR_____ BIKE_____ FOOT/OTHER (Bus- etc.)_____

CLOTHS _____

EXTRA NOTES/OBSERVATIONS ETC

_____

_____

_____

_____

_____

_____

_____

_____

RECORD OF EVENTS

DATE _____ TIME _____ PLACE _____

WHO_____ WHAT_____ WHERE _____

HAIR_____MALE / FEMALE / ANIMAL _____

CAR_____ BIKE_____FOOT/OTHER^(Bus- etc.)_____

CLOTHS _____

EXTRA NOTES/OBSERVATIONS ETC

_____

_____

_____

_____

_____

_____

_____

_____

RECORD OF EVENTS

DATE _____ TIME _____ PLACE _____

WHO_____WHAT_____WHERE _____

HAIR_____MALE / FEMALE / ANIMAL _____

CAR_____ BIKE_____FOOT/OTHER **(Bus- etc.)**_____

CLOTHS _____

EXTRA NOTES/OBSERVATIONS ETC

_____

_____

_____

_____

_____

_____

_____

_____

RECORD OF EVENTS

DATE _____ TIME _____ PLACE _____

WHO_____ WHAT_____ WHERE_____

HAIR_____ MALE / FEMALE / ANIMAL _____

CAR_____ BIKE_____ FOOT/OTHER **(Bus- etc.)**_____

CLOTHS _____

EXTRA NOTES/OBSERVATIONS ETC

_____

_____

_____

_____

_____

_____

_____

_____

RECORD OF EVENTS

DATE _____ TIME _____ PLACE _____

WHO _____ WHAT _____ WHERE _____

HAIR _____ MALE / FEMALE / ANIMAL _____

CAR _____ BIKE _____ FOOT/OTHER^(Bus- etc.) _____

CLOTHS _____

EXTRA NOTES/OBSERVATIONS ETC

_____

_____

_____

_____

_____

_____

_____

_____

RECORD OF EVENTS

DATE _____ TIME _____ PLACE _____

WHO_____ WHAT_____ WHERE _____

HAIR_____ MALE / FEMALE / ANIMAL _____

CAR_____ BIKE_____ FOOT/OTHER **(Bus- etc.)**_____

CLOTHS _____

EXTRA NOTES/OBSERVATIONS ETC

_____

_____

_____

_____

_____

_____

_____

_____

RECORD OF EVENTS

DATE _____ TIME _____ PLACE _____

WHO _____ WHAT _____ WHERE _____

HAIR _____ MALE / FEMALE / ANIMAL _____

CAR _____ BIKE _____ FOOT/OTHER _____
(Bus- etc.)

CLOTHS _____

EXTRA NOTES/OBSERVATIONS ETC

_____

_____

_____

_____

_____

_____

_____

_____

RECORD OF EVENTS

DATE _____ TIME _____ PLACE _____

WHO_____ WHAT_____ WHERE _____

HAIR_____ MALE / FEMALE / ANIMAL _____

CAR_____ BIKE_____ FOOT/OTHER_____ (Bus- etc.)

CLOTHS _____

EXTRA NOTES/OBSERVATIONS ETC

_____

_____

_____

_____

_____

_____

_____

_____

RECORD OF EVENTS

DATE _____ TIME _____ PLACE _____

WHO_____ WHAT_____ WHERE _____

HAIR_____ MALE / FEMALE / ANIMAL _____

CAR_____ BIKE_____ FOOT/OTHER_____
(Bus- etc.)

CLOTHS _____

EXTRA NOTES/OBSERVATIONS ETC

_____

_____

_____

_____

_____

_____

_____

_____

RECORD OF EVENTS

DATE _____ TIME _____ PLACE _____

WHO _____ WHAT _____ WHERE _____

HAIR _____ MALE / FEMALE / ANIMAL _____

CAR _____ BIKE _____ FOOT/OTHER (Bus- etc.) _____

CLOTHS _____

EXTRA NOTES/OBSERVATIONS ETC

_____

_____

_____

_____

_____

_____

_____

_____

RECORD OF EVENTS

DATE _____ TIME _____ PLACE _____

WHO _____ WHAT _____ WHERE _____

HAIR _____ MALE / FEMALE / ANIMAL _____

CAR _____ BIKE _____ FOOT/OTHER _____ (Bus- etc.)

CLOTHS _____

EXTRA NOTES/OBSERVATIONS ETC

_____

_____

_____

_____

_____

_____

_____

_____

_____

RECORD OF EVENTS

DATE _____ TIME _____ PLACE _____

WHO_____ WHAT_____ WHERE _____

HAIR_____ MALE / FEMALE / ANIMAL _____

CAR_____ BIKE_____ FOOT/OTHER (Bus- etc.)_____

CLOTHS _____

EXTRA NOTES/OBSERVATIONS ETC

_____

_____

_____

_____

_____

_____

_____

_____

RECORD OF EVENTS

DATE _____ TIME _____ PLACE _____

WHO_____ WHAT_____ WHERE _____

HAIR_____ MALE / FEMALE / ANIMAL _____

CAR_____ BIKE_____ FOOT/OTHER (Bus- etc.)_____

CLOTHS _____

EXTRA NOTES/OBSERVATIONS ETC

_____

_____

_____

_____

_____

_____

_____

_____

_____

RECORD OF EVENTS

DATE _____ TIME _____ PLACE _____

WHO_____ WHAT_____ WHERE _____

HAIR_____MALE / FEMALE / ANIMAL _____

CAR_____ BIKE_____FOOT/OTHER (Bus- etc.)_____

CLOTHS _____

EXTRA NOTES/OBSERVATIONS ETC

_____

_____

_____

_____

_____

_____

_____

_____

RECORD OF EVENTS

DATE _____ TIME _____ PLACE _____

WHO_____WHAT_____WHERE _____

HAIR_____MALE / FEMALE / ANIMAL _____

CAR_____ BIKE_____FOOT/OTHER^(Bus- etc.)_____

CLOTHS _____

EXTRA NOTES/OBSERVATIONS ETC

_____

_____

_____

_____

_____

_____

_____

_____

RECORD OF EVENTS

DATE _____ TIME _____ PLACE _____

WHO_____ WHAT_____ WHERE _____

HAIR_____MALE / FEMALE / ANIMAL _____

CAR_____ BIKE_____FOOT/OTHER (Bus- etc.)_____

CLOTHS _____

EXTRA NOTES/OBSERVATIONS ETC

_____

_____

_____

_____

_____

_____

_____

_____

RECORD OF EVENTS

DATE _____ TIME _____ PLACE _____

WHO_____ WHAT_____ WHERE _____

HAIR_____ MALE / FEMALE / ANIMAL _____

CAR_____ BIKE_____ FOOT/OTHER _____ (Bus- etc.)

CLOTHS _____

<u>EXTRA NOTES/OBSERVATIONS ETC</u>

_____

_____

_____

_____

_____

_____

_____

_____

RECORD OF EVENTS

DATE _____ TIME _____ PLACE _____

WHO_____ WHAT_____ WHERE _____

HAIR_____ MALE / FEMALE / ANIMAL _____

CAR_____ BIKE_____ FOOT/OTHER _____ (Bus- etc.)

CLOTHS _____

EXTRA NOTES/OBSERVATIONS ETC

_____

_____

_____

_____

_____

_____

_____

_____

RECORD OF EVENTS

DATE _____ TIME _____ PLACE _____

WHO_____ WHAT_____ WHERE _____

HAIR_____ MALE / FEMALE / ANIMAL _____

CAR_____ BIKE_____ FOOT/OTHER _____
                                        (Bus- etc.)

CLOTHS _____

EXTRA NOTES/OBSERVATIONS ETC

_____

_____

_____

_____

_____

_____

_____

_____

RECORD OF EVENTS

DATE _____ TIME _____ PLACE _____

WHO _____ WHAT _____ WHERE _____

HAIR _____ MALE / FEMALE / ANIMAL _____

CAR _____ BIKE _____ FOOT/OTHER (Bus- etc.) _____

CLOTHS _____

EXTRA NOTES/OBSERVATIONS ETC

_____

_____

_____

_____

_____

_____

_____

_____

RECORD OF EVENTS

DATE _____ TIME _____ PLACE _____

WHO_____ WHAT_____ WHERE _____

HAIR_____ MALE / FEMALE / ANIMAL _____

CAR_____ BIKE_____ FOOT/OTHER **(Bus- etc.)** _____

CLOTHS _____

EXTRA NOTES/OBSERVATIONS ETC

_____

_____

_____

_____

_____

_____

_____

_____

RECORD OF EVENTS

DATE _____ TIME _____ PLACE _____

WHO_____ WHAT_____ WHERE _____

HAIR_____ MALE / FEMALE / ANIMAL _____

CAR_____ BIKE_____ FOOT/OTHER **(Bus- etc.)**_____

CLOTHS _____

EXTRA NOTES/OBSERVATIONS ETC

_____

_____

_____

_____

_____

_____

_____

_____

RECORD OF EVENTS

DATE _____ TIME _____ PLACE _____

WHO _____ WHAT _____ WHERE _____

HAIR _____ MALE / FEMALE / ANIMAL _____

CAR _____ BIKE _____ FOOT/OTHER (Bus- etc.) _____

CLOTHS _____

EXTRA NOTES/OBSERVATIONS ETC

_____

_____

_____

_____

_____

_____

_____

_____

_____

RECORD OF EVENTS

DATE _____ TIME _____ PLACE _____

WHO_____ WHAT_____ WHERE _____

HAIR_____ MALE / FEMALE / ANIMAL _____

CAR_____ BIKE_____ FOOT/OTHER_____ (Bus- etc.)

CLOTHS _____

EXTRA NOTES/OBSERVATIONS ETC

_____

_____

_____

_____

_____

_____

_____

_____

_____

RECORD OF EVENTS

DATE _____ TIME _____ PLACE _____

WHO_____WHAT_____WHERE _____

HAIR_____MALE / FEMALE / ANIMAL _____

CAR_____ BIKE_____FOOT/OTHER (Bus- etc.) _____

CLOTHS _____

EXTRA NOTES/OBSERVATIONS ETC

_____

_____

_____

_____

_____

_____

_____

_____

RECORD OF EVENTS

DATE _____ TIME _____ PLACE _____

WHO _____ WHAT _____ WHERE _____

HAIR _____ MALE / FEMALE / ANIMAL _____

CAR _____ BIKE _____ FOOT/OTHER **(Bus- etc.)** _____

CLOTHS _____

EXTRA NOTES/OBSERVATIONS ETC

_____

_____

_____

_____

_____

_____

_____

_____

RECORD OF EVENTS

DATE _____ TIME _____ PLACE _____

WHO _____ WHAT _____ WHERE _____

HAIR _____ MALE / FEMALE / ANIMAL _____

CAR _____ BIKE _____ FOOT/OTHER **(Bus- etc.)** _____

CLOTHS _____

EXTRA NOTES/OBSERVATIONS ETC

_____

_____

_____

_____

_____

_____

_____

_____

RECORD OF EVENTS

DATE _____ TIME _____ PLACE _____

WHO_____ WHAT_____ WHERE _____

HAIR_____MALE / FEMALE / ANIMAL _____

CAR_____ BIKE_____FOOT/OTHER (Bus- etc.)_____

CLOTHS _____

EXTRA NOTES/OBSERVATIONS ETC

_____

_____

_____

_____

_____

_____

_____

_____

RECORD OF EVENTS

DATE _____ TIME _____ PLACE _____

WHO _____ WHAT _____ WHERE _____

HAIR _____ MALE / FEMALE / ANIMAL _____

CAR _____ BIKE _____ FOOT/OTHER (Bus- etc.) _____

CLOTHS _____

EXTRA NOTES/OBSERVATIONS ETC

_____

_____

_____

_____

_____

_____

_____

_____

RECORD OF EVENTS

DATE _____ TIME _____ PLACE _____

WHO_____ WHAT_____ WHERE _____

HAIR_____MALE / FEMALE / ANIMAL _____

CAR_____ BIKE_____FOOT/OTHER^(Bus- etc.)_____

CLOTHS _____

EXTRA NOTES/OBSERVATIONS ETC

_____

_____

_____

_____

_____

_____

_____

_____

RECORD OF EVENTS

DATE _____ TIME _____ PLACE _____

WHO _____ WHAT _____ WHERE _____

HAIR _____ MALE / FEMALE / ANIMAL _____

CAR _____ BIKE _____ FOOT/OTHER (Bus- etc.) _____

CLOTHS _____

EXTRA NOTES/OBSERVATIONS ETC

_____

_____

_____

_____

_____

_____

_____

_____

RECORD OF EVENTS

DATE _____ TIME _____ PLACE _____

WHO _____ WHAT _____ WHERE _____

HAIR _____ MALE / FEMALE / ANIMAL _____

CAR _____ BIKE _____ FOOT/OTHER (Bus- etc.) _____

CLOTHS _____

EXTRA NOTES/OBSERVATIONS ETC

_____

_____

_____

_____

_____

_____

_____

_____

RECORD OF EVENTS

DATE _____ TIME _____ PLACE _____

WHO_____ WHAT_____ WHERE _____

HAIR_____ MALE / FEMALE / ANIMAL _____

CAR_____ BIKE_____ FOOT/OTHER_____ (Bus- etc.)

CLOTHS _____

EXTRA NOTES/OBSERVATIONS ETC

_____

_____

_____

_____

_____

_____

_____

_____

RECORD OF EVENTS

DATE _____ TIME _____ PLACE _____

WHO _____ WHAT _____ WHERE _____

HAIR _____ MALE / FEMALE / ANIMAL _____

CAR _____ BIKE _____ **(Bus- etc.)** FOOT/OTHER _____

CLOTHS _____

EXTRA NOTES/OBSERVATIONS ETC

_____

_____

_____

_____

_____

_____

_____

_____

RECORD OF EVENTS

DATE _____ TIME _____ PLACE _____

WHO _____ WHAT _____ WHERE _____

HAIR _____ MALE / FEMALE / ANIMAL _____

CAR _____ BIKE _____ FOOT/OTHER (Bus- etc.) _____

CLOTHS _____

EXTRA NOTES/OBSERVATIONS ETC

_____

_____

_____

_____

_____

_____

_____

_____

RECORD OF EVENTS

DATE _____ TIME _____ PLACE _____

WHO _____ WHAT _____ WHERE _____

HAIR _____ MALE / FEMALE / ANIMAL _____

CAR _____ BIKE _____ FOOT/OTHER _____ (Bus- etc.)

CLOTHS _____

EXTRA NOTES/OBSERVATIONS ETC

_____

_____

_____

_____

_____

_____

_____

_____

RECORD OF EVENTS

DATE _____ TIME _____ PLACE _____

WHO _____ WHAT _____ WHERE _____

HAIR _____ MALE / FEMALE / ANIMAL _____

CAR _____ BIKE _____ FOOT/OTHER _____ (Bus- etc.)

CLOTHS _____

EXTRA NOTES/OBSERVATIONS ETC

_____

_____

_____

_____

_____

_____

_____

_____

RECORD OF EVENTS

DATE _____ TIME _____ PLACE _____

WHO _____ WHAT _____ WHERE _____

HAIR _____ MALE/FEMALE/ANIMAL _____

CAR _____ BIKE _____ FOOT/OTHER (Bus- etc.) _____

CLOTHS _____

EXTRA NOTES/OBSERVATIONS ETC

_____

_____

_____

_____

_____

_____

_____

_____

RECORD OF EVENTS

DATE _____ TIME _____ PLACE _____

WHO_____ WHAT _____ WHERE _____

HAIR_____MALE / FEMALE / ANIMAL _____

CAR_____ BIKE _____FOOT/OTHER_____ (Bus- etc.)

CLOTHS _____

EXTRA NOTES/OBSERVATIONS ETC

_____

_____

_____

_____

_____

_____

_____

_____

RECORD OF EVENTS

DATE _____ TIME _____ PLACE _____

WHO_____ WHAT_____ WHERE _____

HAIR_____ MALE / FEMALE / ANIMAL _____

CAR_____ BIKE_____ FOOT/OTHER_____
(Bus- etc.)

CLOTHS _____

EXTRA NOTES/OBSERVATIONS ETC

_____

_____

_____

_____

_____

_____

_____

_____

RECORD OF EVENTS

DATE _____ TIME _____ PLACE _____

WHO_____ WHAT_____ WHERE _____

HAIR_____MALE / FEMALE / ANIMAL _____

CAR_____ BIKE_____FOOT/OTHER (Bus- etc.)_____

CLOTHS _____

EXTRA NOTES/OBSERVATIONS ETC

_____

_____

_____

_____

_____

_____

_____

_____

RECORD OF EVENTS

DATE _____ TIME _____ PLACE _____

WHO _____ WHAT _____ WHERE _____

HAIR _____ MALE / FEMALE / ANIMAL _____

CAR _____ BIKE _____ FOOT/OTHER (Bus- etc.) _____

CLOTHS _____

EXTRA NOTES/OBSERVATIONS ETC

_____

_____

_____

_____

_____

_____

_____

_____

RECORD OF EVENTS

DATE _____ TIME _____ PLACE _____

WHO _____ WHAT _____ WHERE _____

HAIR _____ MALE / FEMALE / ANIMAL _____

CAR _____ BIKE _____ FOOT/OTHER^(Bus- etc.) _____

CLOTHS _____

EXTRA NOTES/OBSERVATIONS ETC

_____

_____

_____

_____

_____

_____

_____

_____

RECORD OF EVENTS

DATE _____ TIME _____ PLACE _____

WHO_____ WHAT_____ WHERE _____

HAIR_____ MALE / FEMALE / ANIMAL _____

CAR_____ BIKE_____ FOOT/OTHER_____ (Bus- etc.)

CLOTHS _____

EXTRA NOTES/OBSERVATIONS ETC

_____

_____

_____

_____

_____

_____

_____

_____

RECORD OF EVENTS

DATE _____ TIME _____ PLACE _____

WHO_____ WHAT_____ WHERE _____

HAIR_____ MALE/FEMALE/ANIMAL _____

CAR_____ BIKE_____ **(Bus- etc.)** FOOT/OTHER_____

CLOTHS _____

EXTRA NOTES/OBSERVATIONS ETC

_____

_____

_____

_____

_____

_____

_____

_____

RECORD OF EVENTS

DATE _____ TIME _____ PLACE _____

WHO _____ WHAT _____ WHERE _____

HAIR _____ MALE / FEMALE / ANIMAL _____

CAR _____ BIKE _____ FOOT/OTHER (Bus- etc.) _____

CLOTHS _____

EXTRA NOTES/OBSERVATIONS ETC

_____

_____

_____

_____

_____

_____

_____

_____

RECORD OF EVENTS

DATE _____ TIME _____ PLACE _____

WHO_____ WHAT_____ WHERE _____

HAIR_____ MALE / FEMALE / ANIMAL _____

CAR_____ BIKE_____ FOOT/OTHER_____ (Bus- etc.)

CLOTHS _____

EXTRA NOTES/OBSERVATIONS ETC

_____

_____

_____

_____

_____

_____

_____

_____

RECORD OF EVENTS

DATE _____ TIME _____ PLACE _____

WHO_____WHAT_____WHERE _____

HAIR_____MALE / FEMALE / ANIMAL _____

CAR_____ BIKE_____FOOT/OTHER_____
_(Bus- etc.)

CLOTHS _____

EXTRA NOTES/OBSERVATIONS ETC

_____

_____

_____

_____

_____

_____

_____

_____

_____

RECORD OF EVENTS

DATE _____ TIME _____ PLACE _____

WHO_____ WHAT_____ WHERE _____

HAIR_____ MALE / FEMALE / ANIMAL _____

CAR_____ BIKE_____ FOOT/OTHER_____ (Bus- etc.)

CLOTHS _____

EXTRA NOTES/OBSERVATIONS ETC

_____

_____

_____

_____

_____

_____

_____

_____

RECORD OF EVENTS

DATE _____ TIME _____ PLACE _____

WHO_____ WHAT_____ WHERE _____

HAIR_____ MALE / FEMALE / ANIMAL _____

CAR_____ BIKE_____ FOOT/OTHER**(Bus- etc.)**_____

CLOTHS _____

EXTRA NOTES/OBSERVATIONS ETC

_____

_____

_____

_____

_____

_____

_____

_____

_____

RECORD OF EVENTS

DATE _____ TIME _____ PLACE _____

WHO_____ WHAT_____ WHERE _____

HAIR_____ MALE / FEMALE / ANIMAL _____

CAR_____ BIKE_____ FOOT/OTHER (Bus- etc.)_____

CLOTHS _____

EXTRA NOTES/OBSERVATIONS ETC

_____

_____

_____

_____

_____

_____

_____

_____

RECORD OF EVENTS

DATE _____ TIME _____ PLACE _____

WHO _____ WHAT _____ WHERE _____

HAIR _____ MALE / FEMALE / ANIMAL _____

CAR _____ BIKE _____ FOOT/OTHER (Bus- etc.) _____

CLOTHS _____

EXTRA NOTES/OBSERVATIONS ETC

_____

_____

_____

_____

_____

_____

_____

_____

RECORD OF EVENTS

DATE _____ TIME _____ PLACE _____

WHO_____ WHAT_____ WHERE _____

HAIR_____ MALE / FEMALE / ANIMAL _____

CAR_____ BIKE_____ FOOT/OTHER (Bus- etc.) _____

CLOTHS _____

EXTRA NOTES/OBSERVATIONS ETC

_____

_____

_____

_____

_____

_____

_____

_____

RECORD OF EVENTS

DATE _____ TIME _____ PLACE _____

WHO_____ WHAT_____ WHERE _____

HAIR_____ MALE / FEMALE / ANIMAL _____

CAR_____ BIKE_____ **(Bus- etc.)** FOOT/OTHER_____

CLOTHS _____

EXTRA NOTES/OBSERVATIONS ETC

_____

_____

_____

_____

_____

_____

_____

_____

_____

RECORD OF EVENTS

DATE _____ TIME _____ PLACE _____

WHO_____ WHAT_____ WHERE _____

HAIR_____ MALE / FEMALE / ANIMAL _____

CAR_____ BIKE_____ FOOT/OTHER (Bus- etc.)_____

CLOTHS _____

EXTRA NOTES/OBSERVATIONS ETC

_____

_____

_____

_____

_____

_____

_____

_____

RECORD OF EVENTS

DATE _____ TIME _____ PLACE _____

WHO_____WHAT_____WHERE _____

HAIR_____MALE / FEMALE / ANIMAL _____

CAR_____ BIKE_____FOOT/OTHER**(Bus- etc.)**_____

CLOTHS_____

EXTRA NOTES/OBSERVATIONS ETC

_____

_____

_____

_____

_____

_____

_____

_____

RECORD OF EVENTS

DATE _____ TIME _____ PLACE _____

WHO _____ WHAT _____ WHERE _____

HAIR _____ MALE / FEMALE / ANIMAL _____

CAR _____ BIKE _____ FOOT/OTHER _____ (Bus- etc.)

CLOTHS _____

EXTRA NOTES/OBSERVATIONS ETC

_____

_____

_____

_____

_____

_____

_____

_____

RECORD OF EVENTS

DATE _____ TIME _____ PLACE _____

WHO_____ WHAT_____ WHERE _____

HAIR_____ MALE / FEMALE / ANIMAL _____

CAR_____ BIKE _____ FOOT/OTHER _____ (Bus- etc.)

CLOTHS _____

EXTRA NOTES/OBSERVATIONS ETC

_____

_____

_____

_____

_____

_____

_____

_____

RECORD OF EVENTS

DATE _____ TIME _____ PLACE _____

WHO _____ WHAT _____ WHERE _____

HAIR _____ MALE / FEMALE / ANIMAL _____

CAR _____ BIKE _____ FOOT/OTHER ^(Bus- etc.) _____

CLOTHS _____

EXTRA NOTES/OBSERVATIONS ETC

_____

_____

_____

_____

_____

_____

_____

_____

Printed in Dunstable, United Kingdom